To

Johnny
e
Sally

Thank you for
all yudo

Robin

You Can Do It
Overcome Anxiety

You Can Do It
Overcome Anxiety

First steps to living your best life.

By
Rob Chapman

Cover photo from canva.com

ISBN: 9798385547029
Imprint: Independently published

Dedication

To Fee, for your love, your support, your belief.

For you.

Contents:

FORWARD

Most people worry about one of three things: money, health, or relationships.

If you suffer from constantly being worried about one of those three things, I have good news for you! My good friend Rob Chapman has an excellent book to help. Rob's friendly writing style will immediately make you feel comfortable, like you're sitting at the fireplace with a lifelong friend. He's been around plenty of stressful situations, and he knows what helps.

Rob's clear writing style will immediately help you identify the type of anxiety that you're dealing with. That is usually not enough, however. Rob has been teaching, hypnosis, self-hypnosis, and meditation for decades. His knowledge of the subject is vast. I prefer dealing with people with actual real-world experience. Rob is that person.

I appreciate Rob's understanding of breathing techniques and how to make this simple and effective for people. If you want to change your brain, use these techniques and you will immediately feel better.

His chapter on breaking free of limiting beliefs is gold. Most of the time the issues that we deal with are self-imposed. Having a clear understanding of these beliefs as well as affirmations to help you overcome them is very important and will help you a lot.

Rob is an excellent meditative guide. I particularly liked his going on a voyage metaphor. You'll gain a lot from that exercise as I did.

I know when you are swamped with anxiety and worry that it's difficult to think there's ever a way out. Rob's simple and powerful book can help you find the light at the end of that voyage. Don't wait! Invest time in your healing. You'll be a better person for it.

I'm grateful for my friendship with Rob and after you finish his book, he'll be your friend too.

Tim A. Cummins - The Verbal Surgeon
https://verbalsurgery.libsyn.com/

Introduction

Dear friend,

Anxiety, that fluttery feeling in your chest, is a natural response that can help you stay alert and focused. However, when anxiety takes over, it can be paralyzing and hinder your daily life. It can manifest in physical symptoms such as heart palpitations, sweating, and trembling, as well as emotional symptoms such as fear, worry, and panic.

If you are reading this, you are likely one of the many people who struggle with anxiety. It may feel like anxiety controls your life and you are powerless to stop it. But rest assured, you can overcome it. There are various effective techniques you can use to manage and conquer anxiety.

This book will delve into the common forms of anxiety and the underlying causes of this condition. We will explore transformative techniques such as Neuro Linguistic Programming, hypnosis, mindfulness meditation, and relaxation techniques to help you manage and overcome your anxiety.

Through this book, you will learn to challenge negative thoughts and beliefs that contribute to anxiety and replace them with positive and empowering ones. It is not a quick fix or a one-size-fits-all solution, but with time, effort, and patience, you can overcome anxiety and live a more fulfilling and peaceful life.

Whether it is after the first exercise, after working through the book, or a few weeks after reading, you will start to feel less anxious. This book can assist you in living your best life.

Sending you blessings,

Rob

Chapter 1
Understanding Anxiety:
The Basics

Anxiety, my friend, is a subtle yet powerful force that can infiltrate our lives when we least expect it. It arises from a natural instinct designed to protect us from danger, yet when it lingers too long, it can sabotage our daily routines and experiences.

The signs of anxiety can manifest in various ways, from physical sensations such as rapid heartbeat and perspiration, to mental patterns like worry and racing thoughts that can be challenging to shake.

It's vital to recognize that there are multiple types of anxiety, each with its unique symptoms and causes, such as generalized anxiety, social anxiety, panic attacks, and specific phobias.

Fortunately, there are many effective ways to manage anxiety. Through simple lifestyle adjustments, such as prioritizing regular exercise, a healthy diet, and sufficient rest, we can alleviate anxiety symptoms and improve our overall well-being. Through the techniques shared in this book, you will discover how to reclaim control of your thoughts and emotions and reduce anxiety's hold on your life. Remember, anxiety does not define you or your worth as a person. It's merely a facet of your journey, one that can be managed with dedication and patience.

As you embark on this journey, know that practice is key. The more you apply these exercises, the more they will become ingrained in your daily habits, replacing old patterns with new, empowering ones.

If you're struggling with anxiety, it's wise to seek counsel from a trusted medical professional. A hypnotist, a mind coach or a Druid. When I faced a challenging time in my life and suffered from anxiety, I turned to my doctor and took time off work to focus on my mental and emotional health.

Through the methods in this book, I overcame anxiety and moved forward, and I hope you can do the same. Remember, you are not alone in this journey, and with the right tools and guidance, you can conquer anxiety and thrive.

Chapter 2
The Brain Stuff

So, let us look at the brain stuff behind anxiety!

Anxiety, that restless and overwhelming state of mind, is a multifaceted experience that involves both our body and mind. As we journey through life, we encounter challenges and uncertainties that can activate our stress response, leading to a cascade of physiological and psychological symptoms.

One of the key players in anxiety is the amygdala, that small but mighty almond-shaped structure nestled deep within our brain. The amygdala is the guardian of our emotional wellbeing, detecting potential threats in our environment and triggering the body's innate "fight-or-flight" response. When we are anxious, the amygdala becomes hyperactive, sending signals to other parts of the brain to activate our stress response.

The prefrontal cortex, that wise and discerning region of our brain, is also involved in anxiety. Located at the front of our brain, the prefrontal cortex is responsible for our higher cognitive functions such as decision-making, planning, and impulse control. However, when we are anxious, the prefrontal cortex becomes less active, impairing our ability to think rationally and make sound decisions.

But anxiety is not just a matter of our brain's structure and function. It is also intertwined with our memory and emotional regulation, mediated by the hippocampus, another vital brain region. Furthermore, anxiety can activate the hypothalamus and pituitary gland, which release stress hormones such as cortisol and adrenaline, further exacerbating our physical and emotional state.

So, my friend, be gentle with yourself as you navigate the complex landscape of anxiety. Remember that it is not just a matter of willpower or positive thinking, but a complex interplay of our body, mind, and environment. May you find the courage and wisdom to face your fears, and the compassion and grace to navigate this journey with kindness for yourself.

Chapter 3
Breaking Down the Barriers: Understanding the Different Types of Anxiety

You know, anxiety is a natural response to stress or perceived threat. It is a feeling of unease, such as worry or fear, and can be experienced in varying degrees. However, some individuals may experience excessive or chronic anxiety that interferes with their daily functioning.

It is interesting to note that anxiety is often labelled as a disorder, but is it really a disorder? We must recognize that anxiety is a habit that we have learned. It is an activity, a behaviour, something we do when we feel anxious. The good news is that we can unlearn this habit and learn better ways of thinking and behaving that help us live our best lives.

Now, let us take a closer look at the different forms of anxiety.

Generalized Anxiety is characterized by excessive, persistent, and uncontrollable worry about a variety of different things. This type of anxiety can interfere with our ability to relax and let go of our worries, making it difficult to function in daily life. Physical symptoms such as fatigue, muscle tension, and sleep disturbances are also common with GA.

Panic Anxiety is characterized by sudden and unexpected panic attacks. These attacks are intense and often include physical symptoms such as chest pain, shortness of breath, and heart palpitations. Panic attacks can be triggered by a specific situation or occur unexpectedly, making it difficult for individuals experiencing PA to feel safe and in control. As a result, many individuals may begin to avoid situations or places where they fear a panic attack may occur.

Social Anxiety is characterized by excessive fear or anxiety about social situations in which an individual may be judged or evaluated by others. This fear may be specific to certain types of social situations or may be present in all social situations. Individuals experiencing SA may avoid social situations altogether or endure them with intense fear and discomfort. Physical symptoms such as sweating, blushing, and trembling are common with SA.

Obsessive-Compulsive Anxiety is characterized by persistent, intrusive, and unwanted thoughts, images, or impulses (obsessions) that cause anxiety and distress. Individuals experiencing OCA often try to relieve this anxiety by engaging in repetitive and ritualistic behaviours (compulsions) such as excessive hand washing or checking. These behaviours can become time-consuming and interfere with daily life. Individuals with OCD may also experience other symptoms such as perfectionism, indecisiveness, and hoarding.

Post-Traumatic Stress Anxiety is characterized by the re-experiencing of a traumatic event through intrusive memories, nightmares, or flashbacks. Individuals experiencing PTSA may also experience avoidance of situations or people that remind them of the trauma, as well as negative changes in thoughts and mood. Physical symptoms such as hypervigilance, exaggerated startle response, and difficulty sleeping are also common with PTSA.

In conclusion, my friend, anxiety can take many forms and can interfere with your daily functioning. Recognizing the signs and symptoms of anxiety is the first step in overcoming anxiety and improving overall well-being. Remember, anxiety is a habit that can be unlearned. With practice and patience, you can learn to manage your anxiety and live a fulfilling life. And you can find peace and joy on your journey.

Chapter 3
Unpacking Anxiety:
an overview of causes

Anxiety is a natural response to stress that can affect daily life if it becomes persistent and overwhelming. There are a variety of potential causes of anxiety, including genetic, environmental, and psychological factors. Let us explore some of the most common causes of anxiety.

Genetics

Research indicates that anxiety can run in families, implying that genetics play a role in its development. Studies suggest that inherited factors account for roughly 30-40% of the risk of developing anxiety.

Certain genes may make individuals more vulnerable to anxiety by influencing how their brains react to stress. However, anxiety can also be learned behaviour resulting from children imitating their parents.

Brain Chemistry

Neurotransmitters, which are chemicals in the brain that regulate mood, sleep, and other bodily functions, can contribute to anxiety disorders when their levels fluctuate.

Changes in the levels of neurotransmitters such as serotonin, dopamine, and norepinephrine can lead to anxiety disorders. For instance, low levels of serotonin have been linked to depression and anxiety.

Life Events

Life events such as divorce, job loss, illness, or the death of a loved one can trigger anxiety. Trauma, such as physical or sexual abuse, can also lead to anxiety disorders. People who experience such events may develop post-traumatic stress anxiety (PTSA), which is characterized by symptoms such as flashbacks, nightmares, and avoidance of reminders of the trauma.

Personality Traits

Certain personality traits, such as perfectionism, excessive worrying, and a tendency to avoid risk, can increase the risk of developing anxiety. People who are sensitive or have low self-esteem may also be more prone to anxiety.

Medical Conditions

Certain medical conditions, such as thyroid disorders, heart disease, and respiratory illnesses, can cause anxiety symptoms. Chronic pain, digestive disorders, and autoimmune diseases have also been associated with anxiety.

Substance Use

Substance use, such as alcohol or drug abuse, can cause or exacerbate anxiety symptoms. In some instances, anxiety disorders may arise because of substance use or withdrawal.

Environmental Factors

Environmental factors such as stress at work or school, financial problems, or living in an unsafe neighbourhood can contribute to anxiety disorders. People who experience ongoing stress may be more susceptible to developing anxiety symptoms.

In conclusion, anxiety can have various causes. While some people may be more vulnerable to anxiety due to genetic or personality factors, others may develop anxiety as a result of life events, medical conditions, or environmental factors.

Going forward, we will explore some of the methods we will employ to help you take control of your thoughts, impact your brain chemistry, and enhance your quality of life.

Chapter 4
From Panic to Peace:
Approaches to Change

Greetings, my friend. Allow me to share with you some powerful approaches that I have learned from the great masters of change-work. These techniques have helped countless individuals, including myself and my clients, to achieve their goals and improve their overall well-being.

Neuro Linguistic Programming (NLP) is a fascinating psychological approach developed in the 1970s that recognizes the connection between neurological processes, language, and behaviour. By becoming aware of our patterns of thought and behaviour, we can use NLP techniques such as visualization, self-hypnosis, and mental imagery to reprogram ourselves and achieve our desired outcomes.

Although NLP's effectiveness has been debated by some experts, it has been applied in various areas, such as business, education, sports, therapy, and personal development, with remarkable results.

Hypnosis, a closely related technique, is a state of deep relaxation and focused attention that allows us to become more open to suggestion. It is not mind control, and we are always in control and aware of what is happening.

Hypnosis can help us overcome bad habits or reduce anxiety. It can also take place in conversation or through written words, as you continue reading this book and discover new ways to reduce stress, overcome anxiety, and live your best life.
Meditation is a timeless practice that involves focusing the mind on a particular object, thought, or activity to achieve a state of calmness and relaxation.

Meditation has gained widespread popularity in recent years as a secular practice that can help us reduce stress and anxiety, improve our focus and concentration, and enhance our overall well-being. It can also reduce symptoms of depression and improve mood, making it a useful tool for managing mental health conditions.

Self-hypnosis is another powerful technique that involves inducing a trance-like state in oneself for the purpose of achieving a particular goal or outcome. By using guided imagery, visualization, and suggestion, we can access our subconscious mind and make positive changes. Self-hypnosis can be used to reduce stress and anxiety, improve confidence and self-esteem, overcome phobias and addictions, and enhance performance in sports or other activities. It can be easily learned and practiced at home, making it a convenient and cost-effective way to improve our mental and emotional well-being.

As we journey towards personal change, it is important to identify the approach that works best for our individual needs and commit to the process over the long-term. By empowering ourselves with these techniques, we can tap into our inner resources and make lasting changes that improve the quality of our lives. May you be blessed with the courage and strength to embark on this journey of self-discovery and transformation.

Chapter 5
Soothe Your Anxious Mind: Practical Techniques for a Calmer You

Anxiety is a condition that can imprison the soul, robbing us of the joy and fulfilment that should be ours in this life. It is a thief that steals away our sense of calm and control, leaving us adrift in a sea of fear and uncertainty. But fear not, my friend, for there are techniques that can help us to escape the grip of anxiety and reclaim our lives.

One such technique is the simple act of deep breathing.

Yes, I know what you're thinking - "I've tried that before, and it didn't work!"

But hear me out. When we are anxious, our breathing becomes shallow and rapid, which only serves to exacerbate our feelings of stress and tension. By taking slow, deep breaths, we can signal to our body that it is safe to relax and release the physical symptoms of anxiety.

Yet, when we are in the throws of a panic attack, the thought of counting breaths can feel overwhelming. And the likely hood is that the last thing you will want to do is breathe deeply, and I agree. Once you are having a panic attack it is to late. Unfortunately, we are never told how to use breathing exercises properly to help with anxiety. They work best as prevention than a cure. Practice them daily however you feel, and you will notice the benefits in moments where you used to feel anxious. So let us take a look at the box breathing technique..

By establishing a pattern of controlled breathing - inhaling for a count of four, holding for a count of four, exhaling for a count of four, and holding again for a count of four before repeating the cycle - we can create a soothing rhythm that can help us to overcome even the most intense feelings of anxiety.

Of course, as with any new technique, it may take some time to fully integrate box breathing into your daily routine. Start with a count of four, and gradually increase the length of each breath as you become more comfortable. And don't be afraid to practice this technique throughout the day, even when you are not feeling anxious. By doing so, you can help to lower your overall levels of stress and tension, making it easier to manage any future bouts of anxiety that may come your way.

In the back of this book you will notice a QR code or the website address that will take you to a section on my website where you can watch videos in which I will take you through some of the techniques in the book to help you get the hang of them. There will also be a couple of extra bonus videos in there for you.

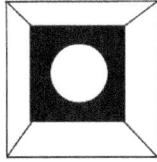

Chapter 6
Box Breathing

Box breathing is a simple yet effective technique that can help you manage and overcome anxiety. This technique involves breathing in for a count of four, holding your breath for a count of four, breathing out for a count of four, and holding your breath for a count of four before starting the cycle again. This creates a rhythm of even and controlled breathing, which can help you relax and calm your mind.

When you first start to practice start with a 4 count, but as you get more experienced you can increase the count, just keep the timing even. I teach this technique to the members of IMeditate, and they are always surprised at how quickly it makes a difference, so do not be surprised when you try this if after a couple of minutes, you can feel more relaxed.

Method:

- To use box breathing to overcome anxiety, find a quiet and comfortable place where you can sit or lie down without any distractions.
- Close your eyes and take a deep breath in through your nose, filling your lungs with air.
- Hold your breath for a count of four, then slowly exhale through your mouth for a count of four.
- Hold your breath for another count of four before starting the cycle again.
- Repeat this for just a couple of minutes the first couple of times building up to several minutes, focusing on your breath and allowing yourself to relax.

As you practice box breathing, you may find it helpful to visualize each step of the process. For example, you might imagine drawing a square with each inhale, hold, exhale, and hold. You can also combine box breathing with other relaxation techniques, such as progressive muscle relaxation or guided imagery, to enhance its effects. You can combine it with a yogic mudra (hand gesture) to help intensify the relaxation as well.

With practice, box breathing can become a powerful tool for managing anxiety and promoting relaxation. Practice it daily a few times a day. Get used to doing it anywhere.

- In bed
- On the loo
- In a queue
- Whilst walking
- Whilst reading
- Whilst watching TV
- Whilst doing house work

Do not limit yourself. After a couple of weeks of using this, you will begin to notice your anxiety is less.

WARNING: Just because this technique will make you feel better do not stop using it once you begin to notice this. Relaxation is good for you so keep doing it and feel good.

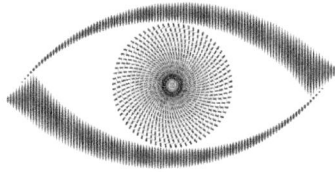

Chapter 7
Erickson's Eyes

This method I have been using with my clients for several years and it is great to now be sharing it with you.

I call it Erickson's Eyes as it combines a technique from the great American hypnotist Milton Erickson with eye movements to help you relax and reduce anxiety. Done daily this method will really make a difference to you. It is powerful and the more you repeat this technique the deeper and more intense the experience can become for you.

Method.

Here's a simple method to combine the Betty Erickson Method of Self-Hypnosis with eye movement from the Havening Technique to reduce anxiety:

1. Find a quiet and comfortable place where you won't be disturbed for a few minutes.

2. Jot down on a piece of paper how anxious you are feeling on a scale of 1-10.

3. Take three deep breaths.

4. Keeping your eyes open for now name to yourself three things that you can see. Now close your eyes
5. Now name three things that you can hear.

6. Now name three things you can feel.

7. Now open your eyes and move them from right to left, keeping your head still. Repeat several times.

8. Whilst moving your eyes right to left, repeat aloud. Either "I am calm and at peace." Or "I release my anxiety and embrace calmness." Do this 10 times.

9. Now repeat the process this time however only name 2 things that you can see. Then close your eye. Two things you can hear, followed by two things you can feel.

Chapter
10. Repeat steps 7 and 8.

11. Now repeat from step 4 again but this time just name 1 thing you see, close your eyes and name one you can hear and one you can see.

12. Repeat steps 7 to 8.

13. Now close your eye gently and just let yourself drift and enjoy the feelings of calm.

14. When you are ready return. Open your eyes and take a few moments to ground yourself. Stretch your body, take a sip of water, and acknowledge the progress you've made in reducing your anxiety.

Remember, this is just one technique of many. As we are all different some techniques you will find come easy, some really easy and some you may have to work a little longer on, but it is worth the effort to reduce your anxiety now and a enjoy your best life.

WARNING: When using techniques do not compare your results one day to the next. You are not the same person each day and therefore neither should you expect your results to be. All that matters is that you begin to notice that anxiety number from 1-10 coming down the more you do this.

Chapter 8
The Imagined Dance

This is the final method in this part of the book.

When it comes to overcoming anxiety the imagination is one of the most powerful tools that you can use. Let's face it, you have been imaging all the potential things that could go wrong and created your anxiety. So let's use that power now to release your anxiety and have you feeling calmer and more relaxed.

Before you have a go at this one let me just mention visualisation. I will keep it simple.

If I were to ask you to think of an apple, what colour is it?

If it was on a table in front of you, would it be to the right, left or the middle?

If we were together in person I dare say you would have found it easy to give me the answers to those two questions. And that my dear friend is what I mean when I say visualisation, just think about it however you do that. Nothing in this book is difficult, but it all works powerfully for you.

Method

1. Find a quiet, comfortable place where you won't be interrupted. Sit in a comfortable position and close your eyes.

2. On piece of paper jot down how anxious you feel on a scale of 1-10.

3. Take three deep breaths, and just become aware of a place within you that feel is most relaxed. Could be anywhere, once located allow that feeling to spin within you. Do this for a minute or two as you relax.

4. Imagine that you are physically moving your body in a way that feels natural to you. This could mean imagining yourself shaking your arms and legs, jumping up and down, or doing a quick dance. Repeat this visualization for a few minutes. If you find that you physically respond then allow the movement to happen.

5. Begin box breathing. Inhale through your nose for a count of 4, hold your breath for a count of 4, exhale through your mouth for a count of 4, and hold your breath for a count of 4. Repeat this cycle for a few minutes.

6. As you visualize yourself moving and practice box breathing, recall a specific memory or trigger that is causing you anxiety. Allow yourself to fully experience the feelings and physical sensations associated with this memory or trigger.

7. Begin to visualize the memory or trigger while moving your eyes back and forth horizontally. Keeping your head still.

8. While continuing to move your eyes back and forth, repeat a statement that acknowledges your anxiety and sets an intention to release it. For example, you could say "Even though I feel anxious about this situation, I choose to release this anxiety and feel calm and centered."

9. As you continue to visualize the memory or trigger, practice box breathing and move your eyes back and forth. Allow the feelings and physical sensations associated with the memory or trigger to come up but, focus on the statement you're repeating and the calming effects of the box breathing and eye movement.

10. Take a few more deep breaths, and imagine yourself feeling calm, centered, and in control. Repeat the statement from step 6 as needed.

11. When you are ready, slowly open your eyes and take a moment to ground yourself before continuing with your day calmer and more relaxed.

12. Check in with yourself, on a scale of 1-10 how much less is your anxiety now?

WARNING: These methods and techniques can create powerful changes in your life, reducing your anxiety and improving your quality of life. However, if you read the book once and then give a halfhearted attempt at the exercises you will not get the most from them. I truly believe that you are worth the time you will find to put into yourself after reading this book.

Chapter 9
Breaking Free from Limiting Beliefs

In order to live a fulfilling life, it's important to identify and overcome the limiting beliefs that hold us back. These beliefs are the negative thoughts and ideas we hold about ourselves and the world around us. They are often formed early in life, and can be difficult to shake off as we get older.

Limiting beliefs can be particularly problematic when it comes to anxiety. Anxiety is often fuelled by worry and fear, and limiting beliefs can amplify those emotions. If we believe that we're not good enough, that we're doomed to fail, or that the world is a dangerous place, we're likely to experience more anxiety than if we had more positive beliefs.

The first step in breaking free from limiting beliefs is to identify them. What negative thoughts do you find yourself having on a regular basis? Do you believe that you're not smart enough, not attractive enough, or not worthy of love and respect? Do you think that success is impossible, or that the world is a dangerous and unpredictable place?

Once you've identified your limiting beliefs, it's important to challenge them. Ask yourself if they're true. Are you not smart enough, or are you just telling yourself that? Is success impossible, or are you just afraid to try? Often, we find that our limiting beliefs are based on faulty assumptions or outdated information. When we challenge them, we can begin to see things in a more positive light.

It's also helpful to replace limiting beliefs with more positive, empowering beliefs. For example, if you've always believed that you're not good enough, try replacing that belief with the idea that you are capable and deserving of success. If you've always thought that the world is a dangerous place, try telling yourself that the world is full of opportunities and adventure.

Breaking free from limiting beliefs can take time, we usually have more than one, but it's essential if we want to live a happy and fulfilling life. By identifying our negative thoughts and challenging them, we can begin to see things in a more positive light. And by replacing limiting beliefs with more empowering ones, we can begin to live the life we truly want.

So are you ready to explore the power of overcoming limiting beliefs and finding freedom from anxiety? Often, we allow our own beliefs and fears to hold us back from living the life we truly desire.

But you can break free from these self-imposed limitations and open yourself up to a world of endless possibilities? By learning to recognize and challenge your limiting beliefs, you can unlock our full potential and live a life of greater joy, peace, and fulfilment.

It's time to let go of the anxiety and step into a new, empowering way of living. So let's journey on to the next section of this book of self-discovery and transformation as we explore the power of overcoming limiting beliefs.

Chapter 10
Limiting Beliefs: Identity Parade

Limiting beliefs can be like invisible barriers that prevent us from achieving our goals and living a fulfilling life. These beliefs are often formed early on in our lives and can be deeply ingrained in our subconscious minds. However, with awareness and practice, we can learn to recognize and break free from these limitations.

One way to recognize limiting beliefs is to pay attention to your self-talk. Notice the thoughts that come up when you are faced with a challenge or opportunity. Are they positive and encouraging, or are they negative and critical? If you find yourself thinking things like "I'm not good enough" or "I'll never be able to do that," these are signs of limiting beliefs that are holding you back.

Another way to recognize limiting beliefs is to examine the patterns in your life. Do you find yourself repeatedly facing the same challenges or situations? Are there areas of your life where you feel stuck or unable to make progress? These can be indications of underlying limiting beliefs that are keeping you trapped in old patterns.

It's important to remember that recognizing limiting beliefs is not about self-judgment or blame. Rather, it's about developing awareness and compassion for ourselves as we work to break free from these limitations. With practice, we can learn to identify and challenge our limiting beliefs, replacing them with more empowering and positive thoughts that help us live the life we truly desire. So, take a deep breath, open yourself up to possibility, and let go of those old, limiting beliefs that are holding you back.

THE ID PARADE:

Below is a list of 22 of the most common limiting beliefs. See it as an ID parade, there they all are lined up and you want to spot which ones are responsible. By that I mean, you want to identify the ones that are holding you back from overcoming anxiety.

There are common themes amongst them. These tend to start with,

I can't……
I don't……
I would but……
I have tried…..
I am not….

Pay attention to your thoughts, begin to notice when these statements appear and make a note of them.

The List

- "I'm not good enough"
- "I'm not smart enough"
- "I don't deserve success/happiness/love"
- "Money is the root of all evil"
- "I'm too old/young to do _____"
- "It's too late to change"
- "I'm not attractive enough"
- "I don't have enough time/money/resources"

- "Success is only for lucky people"
- "I'm not talented enough"
- "I'll never be able to do it"
- "I don't have the right connections/opportunities"
- "People will judge me if I fail"
- "It's not safe to take risks"
- "I'm not worthy of love and respect"
- "I'm a victim of my circumstances"
- "It's selfish to put myself first"
- "I'll never be able to overcome my fears"
- "I'm not capable of achieving my dreams"
- "I'm not meant to be successful/happy/fulfilled"
- It is just who I am
- I can't do it

Once you have identified the limiting beliefs that keep you stuck with your anxiety and that keep it going use the upcoming two step process to really begin to break them down and be free of your limiting beliefs.

Chapter 11
Busting the Belief.... 2 Steps

Limiting beliefs that are not really true tend to not stand up to much once confronted and challenges. In fact, often a limiting beliefs can crumble very quickly when we actually look at the facts. Here is a 2 step method for busting those limiting beliefs.

Step 1: Challenging limiting beliefs

Identify the limiting belief: Start by identifying the belief that is holding you back. For example, "I am not good enough to pursue a particular career." Question the belief: Ask yourself why you believe that. Is there any evidence to support it? Is it a fact or just an opinion?

Gather evidence that contradicts the belief: Look for evidence that contradicts the belief, such as your accomplishments and achievements in related fields, positive feedback from others, and examples of people with similar backgrounds who have succeeded in that career.

Challenge the belief: Use the evidence you've gathered to challenge the belief. For example, "I have achieved success in related fields, received positive feedback, and other people with similar backgrounds have succeeded in this career. Therefore, my belief that I am not good enough is not true."

Step 2: Reframing limiting beliefs

Identify the limiting belief: Start by identifying the belief that is holding you back. For example, "I am not good enough to pursue a particular career." Reframe the belief: Instead of saying "I am not good enough," reframe the belief in a more empowering and positive way. For example, "I am capable of learning and growing in this area," or "I have valuable skills and experience to bring to this career." Repeat the reframed belief: Repeat the reframed belief to yourself regularly, as this will help to reinforce the new, positive mindset.

Remember that it takes time and effort to bust a limiting belief, and it may require ongoing work to maintain a positive mindset. However, with consistent practice and dedication, it is possible to overcome limiting beliefs and achieve your goals.

Chapter 12
Celtic Belief Breakthrough

As someone who has spent almost thirty years studying Druidry & Celtic Spirituality I often find imagery within the tradition that helps with the change work that I practice with my clients. Here is a favorite of mine for Installing a new belief.

Identify the limiting belief: In order to overcome a limiting belief, first take a moment to identify what it is that holds you back. This could be something like "I am not capable" or "I don't deserve happiness."

Write down the limiting belief: Once you have recognized your limiting belief, write it down on a piece of paper or in a journal. This helps to bring it out of your mind and into the physical world, making it easier to confront.

Challenge the belief: Begin to challenge the belief by questioning it. Ask yourself, "Is this belief really true?" or "Where did this belief come from?" This inquiry can help to give you a new perspective and shift your mindset.

Reframe the belief: Once you have challenged your limiting belief, it's time to reframe it into a positive statement. Transform "I am not capable" to "I am capable and worthy of success." This new statement will help you to feel empowered and motivated.

Use hypnosis to reinforce the new belief:
(You will learn more about using hypnosis later on in the book.)

Find a quiet space where you can relax and enter a state of meditation/trance. Visualize a serene landscape, somewhere in nature that feels comforting to you. As you imagine yourself in this place, you discover a standing stone. Placing your hands upon the stone you become aware of an energy in it, this energy starts to resonate in you. Where do you begin to feel that? Allow it to spin within you. Now, repeat your new positive statement. This will help to embed the belief deep into your subconscious. Allowing the new belief to be fuelled by the energy from the stone.

Once you feel filled with that energy and the new belief. Stop, and take a moment to picture the new you, free from that old limiting belief. Then drift into that you. See what that you sees, hear what that you hears and sense and know all that you knows that allows you to be that you now.

Practice the new belief: Repeat your new positive statement throughout the day. Take actions that align with your new belief and celebrate your successes. You will be surprised at how quickly your mindset shifts and how much more capable you feel.

Chapter 13
Metaphorical Transformation

The technique is called "metaphorical transformation" and it involves transforming the limiting belief into a metaphorical representation, then transforming that representation into a more empowering and positive one.

To use this technique, follow these steps:

Identify the limiting belief:

First, identify the limiting belief that is holding you back.

Transform the belief into a metaphor:

Next, transform the limiting belief into a metaphorical representation. For example, if the limiting belief is "I'm not good enough", the metaphorical representation could be a heavy weight that you are carrying around.

A metaphor is a figure of speech that compares two things in a way that is not literally true but is used to explain an idea or concept. In self-help work, metaphors can be powerful tools for understanding and transforming one's thoughts and behaviours. They can help people visualize their experiences and emotions in a new light, and offer a way to express complex ideas in a simple and relatable way.

For example, the metaphor of a journey can be used to describe the process of personal growth and development, with its ups and downs, detours, and milestones. By using metaphors, self-help writers and practitioners can help readers and clients gain insights into themselves, their relationships, and their lives, and empower them to make positive changes.

Examine the metaphor: Take some time to explore the metaphor and understand it better. What does the weight represent? Why is it so heavy? What purpose does it serve?

Transform the metaphor: Once you have a better understanding of the metaphor, transform it into a more empowering and positive representation. For example, you could imagine yourself lifting the weight effortlessly or transforming it into a feather that you can easily carry.

Repeat the new metaphor: Finally, repeat the new metaphor to yourself regularly, until it becomes your new belief.

By using the metaphorical transformation technique, you are tapping into the power of your subconscious mind to create a powerful and lasting change. This technique has the potential to be a powerful tool in overcoming limiting beliefs and in turn anxiety. I wonder how much better you can feel if you were to use the same method but instead of a limiting belief use a metaphor for your anxiety and discover how you can let it go.

In the depths of anxiety's grip, it can be easy to lose sight of the horizon and feel trapped in the present moment. The mind becomes consumed by worry, doubts and fears. But like a great tree that endures storms and seasons, we too can withstand the tempests of anxiety by grounding ourselves in a sense of purpose and direction.

Within the Druidic tradition that I belong to we are reminded that goals are the compass by which we navigate the seas of uncertainty, helping us to stay true to our course even in the roughest of waters.

The mystical wisdom of the Celtic tradition reveals that the future is not a foregone conclusion, but an open field of possibility that we can shape with our intentions and actions. As we embark on the journey towards overcoming anxiety, we can take solace in the knowledge that the path ahead is not set in stone, but a canvas awaiting our creative touch.

Let's pause to look at a story from the Celtic tradition on our journey to overcome anxiety.

Chapter 14
St Brendan, The Voyager.

In the ancient Celtic tale of St Brendan the Voyager, we find a story of hope and perseverance in the face of great uncertainty.

Brendan and his crew set out on a journey across the vast and tumultuous sea, facing many trials and tribulations along the way. But despite the storms and perils that beset them, Brendan never lost sight of his ultimate goal – the discovery of the fabled "Land of Promise". He and his crew were guided by a sense of purpose that kept them moving forward, even in the darkest of moments.

The story of St Brendan is a powerful metaphor for the journey of overcoming anxiety. Like Brendan and his crew, we too face storms and uncertainty in our lives. Anxiety can feel like a tempest that threatens to capsize us at any moment. But by anchoring ourselves to a sense of purpose and direction, we can weather these storms and navigate our way towards a brighter horizon.

The Celtic tradition teaches us that the journey itself can be a source of transformation and growth. Every trial and tribulation we face can be an opportunity for learning and self-discovery. And when we keep our sights set on our ultimate goals, we can find the strength and resilience to keep moving forward, even when the way ahead seems treacherous.

In the end, the story of St Brendan the Voyager reminds us that the journey of overcoming anxiety is not an easy one, but it is a journey that is worth taking. By setting our sights on the horizon and committing ourselves to our goals, we can find the courage and determination to face whatever challenges come our way, and emerge stronger and more resilient than before.

In the next few chapters, we will explore practical methods for harnessing the power of goals to move beyond anxiety's grip and discover the potential that lies within us.

Chapter 15
Voyage to Overcome Anxiety

This exercise is designed to help you let go of anxiety and build a focus that will help you achieve the goals you will be setting.

You may wish to just follow it as you read it and this will work well for you, or you may choose to record it and listen back, whichever you choose to overcome anxiety and achieve your goals. I know you will enjoy this.

- As you settle into a comfortable position, let your mind become open and receptive to the words that follow. Notice how your mind can drift and wander, as if floating on a gentle sea.

- Imagine yourself on a voyage, facing challenges and trials along the way. Like Brendan and his crew, you may encounter storms that test your mettle and push you to your limits.

- But as you journey onward, notice how a sense of purpose and direction begins to guide you, like a beacon shining in the night. This purpose, this sense of direction, can be your anchor, keeping you steady and focused no matter what challenges come your way.

- With each trial and tribulation, you become stronger and more resilient, like a ship weathering the storm. You know that every step you take is bringing you closer to the life you truly desire, a life filled with greater peace and fulfilment.

- So repeat these affirmations to yourself, with conviction and determination:

- "I have the courage and determination to weather any storm. Each step I take brings me closer to a life of greater peace and fulfilment."

- Take a deep breath, and as you exhale, allow yourself to feel stronger and more resilient than ever before. Count slowly to three, and as you emerge from this exercise, notice how you feel more relaxed, more focused, and more in tune with your purpose.

- You can repeat this exercise as often as you like, each time allowing yourself to become more deeply relaxed and more closely attuned to your inner guidance. As you journey onward, may you find strength and purpose in every step you take.

Chapter 16
The Power of Emotional Goals

It is often at this point that you find the usual goal setting advice of setting smart goals, of things you want to achieve in the world. But anxiety is not in the world, it is within you. The problem with goals out there is that things can often get in the way. The only thing you really have any control in this world is your thoughts and feelings. What you want to tell yourself about your experience and how you want to feel about it, and that my friend is where Emotional Goals come in.

Our emotions are the one thing we have complete control over. They can shape our entire perception of the world around us, and they have the power to either empower or hinder us from achieving our dreams. That's why setting emotional goals is so important.

When we set emotional goals, we're not just setting out to achieve external milestones, like a new job or a bigger house. Instead, we're focusing on the internal experiences we want to have - the emotions that we want to feel on a regular basis. By setting emotional goals, we can take control of our emotional state and create a life that is rich with positive emotions like joy, fulfilment, and love.

The benefits of setting emotional goals are numerous. For starters, when we focus on the emotions we want to feel, we're less likely to get distracted by external circumstances that are outside of our control. This means that we can feel happy and fulfilled even when things don't go exactly as planned.

Furthermore, setting emotional goals can help us break free from negative emotional patterns. For example, if we tend to feel anxious or depressed, we can set a goal to feel calm and content instead. By focusing on this goal, we can begin to shift our internal state and create new emotional habits that serve us better.

So how do we go about setting and achieving emotional goals?

Chapter 17
The Emotional Goal-Setting Method

Step 1 - Identify the emotions you want to feel. Start by asking yourself, "What emotions do I want to experience on a regular basis?" Write down your answers in a journal or on a piece of paper.

Step 2 - choose one or two emotions that you want to focus on. These will be your emotional goals. Make sure they are specific emotions, such as joy, confidence, or peace, and not vague concepts like "happiness."
Once you've identified your emotional goals, it's time to get to work.

Here's a powerful method for achieving your emotional goals:

- Imagine yourself already feeling the emotion you want to achieve. Use all of your senses to imagine what it feels like to experience that emotion fully. What does it look like? Sound like? Feel like?

- Identify the actions and behaviours that would naturally lead to you feeling that emotion. For example, if your emotional goal is to feel confident, you might identify behaviours like speaking up in meetings or trying new things.

- Start taking those actions and behaviours on a daily basis. Even small steps can make a big difference. Each time you take an action that is aligned with your emotional goal, you're training your brain to associate that behaviour with the emotion you want to feel.

- Celebrate your progress along the way. When you start to feel the emotion you're aiming for, take a moment to celebrate your progress. Recognize that you're creating new emotional habits and that you have the power to continue doing so.

Using this method, you can achieve your emotional goals and create a life filled with positive emotions. Remember, your emotions are within your control, and you have the power to shape your emotional state in any way you choose.

Chapter 18
The Two Practices I Love the Most

This is the penultimate chapter in this book. I wanted to make sure you explored the techniques rather than got lost in information and I do hope that this has worked for you.

I mentioned earlier that I have ridden the wave of anxiety myself. Indeed, I first had to really deal with when I discovered that I could not have children. An operation I had several years previous to finding out and basically blocked the exit and so even though I was fertile I was producing a 0 count. I thought I could deal with this information, however, I started to experience anxiety and was unable to cope with life for a while.

At the time I was training as a counsellor and so I went to my Doctor and told him that I did not want pills but time and space to get my head around it all.

He signed me off for a month, which gave me the space I needed. There are three things that got me back on track, the Wisdom of the Druidic & Celtic Path, Meditation and Self Hypnosis. The latter two of which we will explore next.

Meditation and self-hypnosis are powerful tools that can help individuals overcome anxiety. By practicing these techniques, individuals can learn to calm their minds, reduce stress, and develop a greater sense of inner peace.

Meditation is a practice that involves focusing your attention on a particular object, thought, or activity to achieve a state of mental clarity and emotional calm. Research has shown that regular meditation can help reduce symptoms of anxiety, depression, and stress. It can also improve overall mood and promote feelings of well-being.

Self-hypnosis, on the other hand, is a technique that involves inducing a state of deep relaxation and heightened suggestibility in oneself. During a self-hypnosis session, individuals can use positive affirmations and visualizations to help them overcome anxiety and other emotional challenges.

One of the key benefits of meditation and self-hypnosis is that they can help individuals develop greater self-awareness. By becoming more aware of their thoughts and emotions, individuals can learn to recognize when they are experiencing anxiety and take steps to manage it before it becomes overwhelming.

Another benefit of these techniques is that they can help individuals develop greater resilience in the face of stress and adversity. By practicing meditation and self-hypnosis regularly, individuals can learn to remain calm and centred in challenging situations, allowing them to respond more effectively to stressful events.

Finally, meditation and self-hypnosis can help individuals cultivate a greater sense of inner peace and well-being. By learning to quiet their minds and focus on the present moment, individuals can develop a deeper sense of connection to themselves and the world around them, leading to a greater sense of purpose and meaning in their lives.

In conclusion, if you are struggling with anxiety, meditation and self-hypnosis can be valuable tools to help you overcome it. By practicing these techniques regularly, you can learn to manage your emotions more effectively, develop greater resilience, and cultivate a greater sense of inner peace and well-being. So why not give them a try and see how they can help you live a happier, more fulfilling life?

Chapter 19
Meditation

Meditation is a timeless practice that has been passed down through the ages, originating in the ancient traditions of India and the East. It is a way of training the mind to focus and find stillness, enabling us to access a deeper level of awareness and consciousness.

At its essence, meditation is about cultivating a sense of inner peace and harmony, and connecting with the present moment. In our fast-paced, technology-driven world, it can be difficult to quiet the mind and find a sense of calm, but meditation offers a powerful antidote to the stresses and distractions of modern life.

There are many different forms of meditation, from mantra-based practices to breathwork and visualization techniques. Some people meditate in silence, while others use guided meditations or listen to music to help them enter a state of relaxation and concentration.

There are however a lot of myths that stop people from enjoying meditation. This is partly why I started IMeditate, to break down the myths and beliefs that get in the way for people.

- **I Have to Empty my Mind and Stop thinking:**
All I will say here is that the only time you
stop thinking as a human being is when you
are dead and none of us want to rush that.
You are human, you think, it is what we do.

  Now, let me ask you, have you ever been in a
conversation with someone where your
attention is grabbed for a moment by
something else and for those moments you
no longer hear the person? We all have, and
that is what you want to do with your
thoughts, just focus more on what you are
doing than what you are thinking. Like a radio
in the background, the more you focus on
your meditation practice the easier it
becomes. What if those thoughts keep
coming? Well, use them as your meditation.

  At it's simplest meditation is focusing on one
thing until that is all you are focusing on. A
guided meditation could just as easily be
around a supermarket shopping as a
woodland walk.

- **I can't visualize:**

  If I say to you, " A Big Blue Buss, Drove up the
Grey Road, and passed the Yellow House. "
Do you know what I am talking about? Yes,
Good, that means you can visualize.

To know what I am describing in that sentence your mind accesses the images that you have associated to the words, otherwise you would not know what I meant. Some of us, probably about 60% of people have a filter that stops that image bleeding into conscious awareness, but you are still visualizing. When asked to visualize in meditation just think about it, however you do that, in the same way you may think of a red apple.

I can't relax:

- Yet, and actually, relaxation is a side effect of meditation. So, stop trying to and just allow it. When I teach self-hypnosis I often hear people say that they have difficulty relaxing, 5 minutes later and they are nicely relaxed. We will look at that in the self-hypnosis session.

- **Funky Posture:**

   I can't meditate because you have to hold a difficult position like in the movies. Actually, no, you just need to be sat comfortably in a way that does not restrict your breathing.

Now that we have cleared up some of the most common myths about meditation let me share a really simple method to get you practicing.

Chapter 20
4 Steps to Meditation

1. Get comfy, have a stretch, have a fidget. Take a few deep breaths and then return to your natural breath. Get curious about your breath, how it feels, where it goes and just observe. Do this for about 3-5 minutes.

2. Start to focus on the outbreath, at the final point of the outbreath start to count backward from 19 to 1. Counting down one number for each breath out. Repeat this for about 3-5 minutes. (If counting backwards is a little distracting count up.)

3. Shift focus to your inbreath. At the very last highest point of your inbreath count again. Downward from 19 to 1 Repeat for 3-5 minutes.

4. Shift your focus to your entire breath, follow it as it enters your body, imagine it travelling all the way down to your toes and then back out. Repeat at your natural pace for 3-5 minutes.

In my book you Can Do It – Meditation I explore a number of techniques that you maybe interested in for meditation, however if you only ever used this technique then you would be able to master meditation with time.

A Few Extra Notes

Location – I do not think I have ever read this anywhere else, which does not mean that it is not, but, **practice meditation everywhere**. What use us meditation if you can only ever do it on a lily pad with a certain type of incense and your favorite floaty music?

You should be able to meditate as well in a busy shopping center as by an idyllic lake. Before every practice make this statement.

"I am going to relax, I am going to meditate.

Outside noises will not distract me, everyday thoughts will not disturb me, they pass me by like clouds in the sky."

Saying this before every session overtime will act as a suggestion to your mind and you will be able to meditate almost anywhere. I remember being at a Mind, Body, Spirit fayre once, after setting up I sat for a while in meditation. Afterward people came over to me to say that they were amazed, how could I meditate with everyone setting up all around me. Simple, I gave myself permission to, and for the sounds to be there. The sound of the people setting up their stalls became my meditation.

Meditation Apps – Avoid! If you only ever meditate using an ap the ability to meditate becomes anchored to that action and app. If you are out an do not have access to the app you can find yourself unable to meditate, so avoid them.

Clothing – Loose fitting and warm.

Music – can be nice, but you can become dependent on having music so mix it up a bit. Sometimes with, sometimes without.

Now let us look at Self Hypnosis.

Chapter 21
Self-Hypnosis

Well my friend, I have saved, for me what is the best till last. Self-Hypnosis was the first self-help technique I learnt, believe it or not when I was just ten tears of age. It is a delight to be sharing it with you.

Within the transformative power of self-hypnosis, we have the opportunity to tap into the vast reservoirs of inner strength and wisdom that reside within us. Self-hypnosis is a gentle and effective tool that can help us ease anxiety, cultivate focus, and access the deep well of calm that resides within. By entering a state of deep relaxation and focused awareness, we can quiet the chatter of our conscious minds and tap into the wisdom of our subconscious. With practice, we can learn to harness this inner wisdom and use it to create a more peaceful and fulfilling life.

Through self-hypnosis, we can cultivate a sense of inner peace and resilience that can carry over into all aspects of our lives. By learning to visualize ourselves in peaceful and calming environments, we can shift our focus away from our worries and towards a sense of calm and well-being. With each session of self-hypnosis, we have the opportunity to deepen our connection to ourselves and to the mystery of our own being.

So, dear friend, I invite you to explore the transformative power of self-hypnosis. By tapping into the vast reservoirs of inner strength and wisdom that reside within us, we can create a life that is rich, fulfilling, and deeply meaningful. Let's begin.

You need to be able to sit comfortably and not be disturbed for the allotted time that you choose for your session. And as I tell my students, once ready follow the method that follows, as always, the more you do it, and you can do it, the better your results.

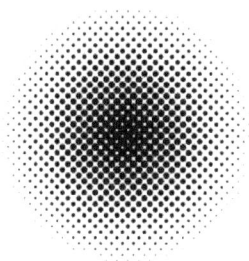

Chapter 22
Simple Steps to Self-Hypnosis

These steps for going into hypnosis are the ones I like to teach my students and appear in my online Self Hypnosis course.

Read through them a few times to become familiar with them and then break it down into each step. Practising until you are familiar.

1. Deep breath, tell yourself I am going to use self-hypnosis, I will be in hypnosis for _____ minutes (no more than 10), outside noises will not distract me, if there is a n emergency I will emerge clear headed, calm and relaxed and able to deal with the situation to the best of my ability.

2. Look at your right arm, Once you can sense and feel it, close your eyes.

3. Relax the arm, tell it to relax, keep relaxing it. Then when it feels deeply relaxed.

4. Imagine a calming and peaceful place.

5. Give your suggestion: " I am mastering the magic of self-hypnosis in my life" (9 times)

6. Drift, let yourself go, do not analyze, do not plan, just sit back and observe your experience of you.

7. Remind yourself, I am feeling calm, peaceful, happy. I have a bright future with the magic of self-hypnosis working powerfully for me.

8. Emerge, count yourself out.

1 – I feel energized, refreshed,
2- Coming back to everyday awareness
3- Take a deep breath, feel good
4-Imagine a refreshing rain, cleansing and clearing
5- Eyes open, feel good stretch.

I would recommend using the suggestion at step 5 for at least a fortnight. You will begin to notice each time how your experience of self-hypnosis intensifies. When you get really good at it you only have to think about going into self-hypnosis and you can, whenever you choose.

After the first few weeks you can change the suggestion for one that follows or create your own. Only ever work with one suggestion at a time to get the most from it.

Chapter 23
20 Powerful Suggestions: Overcome Anxiety and Live Your Best Life

Once you have spent a few weeks using the suggestion in the method for self-hypnosis you can change it for one of the below suggestions. Use one at a time and keep using it for a minimum of 14 days.

- I have the power to overcome anxiety and live a life free of fear.

- Every day, I am becoming more relaxed and confident in myself.

- I am capable of achieving my goals and overcoming any obstacles that come my way.

- My mind and body are becoming more and more calm and centred every day.

- I am able to let go of any negative thoughts or beliefs that no longer serve me.

- I am filled with positive energy and surrounded by loving, supportive people.

- My thoughts are clear and focused, and I am able to make sound decisions.

- I am able to manage stress and stay calm in any situation.

- I am in control of my thoughts and emotions, and I choose to focus on the positive.

- I am confident and self-assured, and I trust in my abilities.

- I am able to face challenges with courage and determination.

- I am worthy of love and respect, and I treat myself with kindness and compassion.

- I am grateful for all of the good things in my life, and I focus on the positive.

- I am able to let go of the past and live in the present moment.

- I am open to new experiences and opportunities, and I embrace change.

- I am constantly growing and evolving, and I am excited for the future.

- I am filled with joy and happiness, and I spread positivity to those around me.

- I am able to connect with others on a deep and meaningful level.

- I am able to find peace and tranquillity within myself, no matter what is happening around me.

- I am living my best life, and I am excited for what the future holds.

The more you practice self-hypnosis the better it will work for you and become a powerful tool for exploring your inner self and transforming your life.

The changes we achieve through hypnosis can feel natural and subtle, yet they really make a difference in your life. As you practice these methods do not be surprised if others start to notice a shift in you before you do.

Chapter 24
Step into Hope

Anxiety is a pervasive problem that can impact every aspect of our lives. It can hold us back from pursuing our dreams, prevent us from enjoying the present moment, and even harm our physical health. But the good news is that anxiety can be overcome, and the process can be quicker than you might expect.

In this book, I have shared with you a variety of techniques that can help you manage your anxiety and take control of your life. From Box breathing to Self-Hypnosis, there are many approaches you can use to reduce your anxiety and increase your resilience.

But here's the thing: reading about these techniques is only the first step. To truly overcome anxiety, you need to put them into practice

This may sound daunting but remember that every journey begins with a single step. And with each step, you'll find yourself becoming more confident, more capable, and more in control.

The key to success is to start small and build momentum. Pick one technique from this book and commit to practicing it consistently for a week. Then, add another technique and continue to build on your progress. Over time, you'll find that you're developing new habits and ways of thinking that support your well-being and resilience.

As someone who believes in the transformative power of change, I have been privileged to help many people overcome their anxieties and find greater fulfilment in their lives. I understand that each person's journey is unique, and I am here to offer support and guidance every step of the way.

Sometimes, the next step is to reach out! I hear from people all over the globe, maybe the next person could be you. If so, I really look forward to hearing from you. If not, I truly hope that the techniques in this little book help transform your life as they have mine.

As you put them into practice, and as you start to notice how you can feel different, be sure to tell others about the book, or even treat them to a copy.

By ourselves we can achieve good things, together we create great things.

Wishing every blessing upon your journey.

Rob.

Recommended Reading

I love reading, how do you share a lifetime of doing so? Here are some titles I recommend.

Wisdom of the Celtic Saints
Edward C. Sellener

The Science of Self-Hypnosis
Adam Eason

Get the Life You Want
Richard Bandler

The Druid Way
Phillip Carr-Gomm

Coming to Wholeness
Connirae Andreas

The Celestine Prophecy
James Redfield

And for something more in depth

Tranceformations
Richard Bandler & John Grinder

The Collected Works Of Milton H Erickson
Milton H Erickson & Earnest Rossi

About the Author

Rob Chapman has been interested in self-help and spirituality since childhood. After seeing a stage hypnotist when he was ten, he began studying books on self-help, the mind, and spirituality. In 1997, he joined the Order of Bards, Ovates, and Druids, completing his training after ten years to become a Druid.

Since then, Rob has continued to study and train as a hypnotist, NLP practitioner, counsellor, and spiritual life coach, in addition to his personal and spiritual development. Over the past 25 years, he has run retreats, workshops, and provided talks on various aspects of self-help, hypnosis, Druidry, and Celtic Spirituality. He is also a qualified meditation teacher and founder of IMeditate, an online self-help community. In 2022, he founded Oak Tree Ministry to help people explore the wisdom of Celtic spirituality.

Rob was inspired to write his latest self-help book after noticing that almost every client who came to him was struggling with anxiety and fear. He wanted to create a book that was quick and easy to access, not overloaded with information, and focused on overcoming anxiety. The techniques he shares in his book draw on his lifetime of experience and powerful methods of personal transformation, providing a practical approach to dealing with anxiety.

Through his book, Rob aims to provide readers with practical tools to overcome anxiety. The book is designed to be easily accessible and convenient, so readers can carry it with them and use it whenever they need it. Drawing on his extensive experience as a hypnotist, meditation teacher, and spiritual life coach, Rob offers readers unique insights and techniques to help them transform their lives.

Rob's qualifications and experiences make him well-suited to write this book. He has mentored with top UK hypnotist Jonathan Chase and studied the work of renowned hypnotists and change workers such as Richard Bandler, Igor Ledochowski, Jerry Kein, Bob Burns, Anthony & Freddy Jacquin, Mike Mandel and Cain Ramsey. He has run international Druid workshops and retreats, authored several books, and has been a speaker for over two decades.

Rob has received positive feedback from those he has worked with who have benefited from his techniques, including Jess Roper, a two-time English kickboxing champion, who said:

"You have a way of guiding people into a deep/internal state where they can access what they need to, to heal. You take me to a very 'deep' level. It's wonderful; it's comforting, and uplifting."

Looking ahead, Rob plans to continue publishing accessible self-help books with the aim of providing simple real-world solutions to everyday challenges. He also continues to work with clients as a hypnotist, meditation teacher and mind coach, helping them to transform their lives and overcome their fears.

You can discover more of Rob's work by visiting:

www.makelifebetter.org.uk

&

www.oaktreeministry.org.uk

You can download audio and video files of most of the exercises in this book and access some extras from Rob by visiting.

www.makelifebetter.org.uk/oa

or by scanning the QR code.

Your Password for accessing this page is:

YCDIOA23

Printed in Great Britain
by Amazon

24044664R00066